7 10

DATE DUE		
DEC 13 2010		
MAR 04 2012		

The Urbana Free Library

To renew materials call
217-367-4057

Getting There

Marla Stewart Konrad

Tundra Books

7/10
13⁰⁰

Published in Canada by Tundra Books,
75 Sherbourne Street, Toronto, Ontario M5A 2P9

Published in the United States by
Tundra Books of Northern New York,
P.O. Box 1030, Plattsburgh, New York 12901

Library of Congress Control Number: 2008903005

Photo credits:

Cover: Large – Jerry Galea
Small, from top to bottom – Violeta Roman, John Kautz,
Sarat Arias and Carlos Brito, Gerta Yzeiraj,
AmioAscension, Lu Fengxian, Justin Douglass,
Jon Warren
Title Page: Jon Warren
Dedication Page: Justin Douglass

Spreads
Walk/Run: Jon Warren, Ann Birch, John Schenk
Ride: Justin Douglass, Jon Warren, Justin Douglass
Bike: Maida Irawani, Sopheak Kong, Albert Yu
School: Faustina Boakye, James East, Evelyn Lopez
Fast/Slow: Justin Douglass
Swim: Johnson Tobing, Sithmini Perera, Jon Warren
Wheels: Katrina Peach, Johnson Tobing, Jon Warren
Pull/Push: Asanga Warnakulasuriya, John Schenk
Being Carried: Alyssa Bistonath, Jon Warren, Philip Maher,
  Jon Warren
Boats: Jon Warren, Sithmini Perera, Andrea Dearborn
Dreams: Jon Warren

Library and Archives Canada Cataloguing in Publication

Stewart Konrad,
    Getting there / Marla Stewart Konrad.
(World vision early reader series)
Target audience: For ages 2-5.
ISBN 978-0-88776-867-5

        1. Transportation--Juvenile fiction. I. Title. II. Series.

PS8621.O55G48 2009   jC813'.6   C2008-902101-0

We acknowledge the financial support of the Government of Canada through the Book Publishing Industry Development Program (BPIDP) and that of the Government of Ontario through the Ontario Media Development Corporation's Ontario Book Initiative. We further acknowledge the support of the Canada Council for the Arts and the Ontario Arts Council for our publishing program.

ONTARIO ARTS COUNCIL
CONSEIL DES ARTS DE L'ONTARIO

Printed and bound in China

1 2 3 4 5 6   14 13 12 11 10 09

In memory of Belinda Green,
whose friendship brought so much joy to the journey

When I have places to go,
there are many different ways
of getting there. I can walk …
or I can run.

I might ride a camel or a horse or a yak

... or pedal a bike.

There are lots of ways of getting to school.
Can you name them?

I can go very fast … or ever so slowly.

I might even decide to swim.

Wheels make getting there easy.

I can pull my friends along with me.
I can push them, too.

Being carried is always nice …

. . . and so is getting there by boat.

When I have places to go, I can always
get there in my dreams. Good night!